ACKNOWLEDGEMENTS
I dedicate this book to those who organised and joined the Black Lives Matter protests following the murder of George Floyd. Special thanks to my partner Baindu Kallon for her constructive feedback and her endless emotional support. Thank you to Colm Bryce for editing the book. I am also grateful to Leo Zeilig, Patricia Rodney, Nigel Westmass, Amanda Kingsley and Anne Braithwaite for their invaluable comments on my draft. I owe a great deal of my political education to the Socialist Workers Party. My comrades in the party have always encouraged me to deepen my theoretical and activist engagement with Marxism.

ABOUT THE AUTHOR
Chinedu Chukwudinma is a socialist activist and writer based in London. He writes on African politics, popular struggles and the history of working class resistance on the continent.

COVER IMAGE: Walter Rodney, in 1976. Reproduced with kind permission of the Water Rodney Foundation. INSIDE FRONT: Walter Rodney addressing a meeting of workers in Guyana INSIDE BACK: Walter Rodney's funeral in Georgetown, Guyana, June 1980

Published by Bookmarks Publications 2022
Copyright Bookmarks, 1 Bloomsbury Street, London WC1B 3QE
ISBN print edition: 978-1-914143-05-2
ISBN Kindle: 978-1-914143-06-9
ISBN ePub: 978-1-914143-07-6
ISBN PDF: 978-1-914143-08-3

Series design by Noel Douglas
Typeset by Colm Bryce and Simon Guy for Bookmarks Publications
Printed by Halstan & Co Ltd, Amersham, England

A Rebel's Guide to
WALTER RODNEY

CHINEDU CHUKWUDINMA

ALSO IN THIS SERIES:
A Rebel's Guide to Friedrich Engels by Camilla Royle
A Rebel's Guide to Alexandra Kollantai by Emma Davis
A Rebel's Guide to Orwell by John Newsinger
A Rebel's Guide to James Connolly by Sean Mitchell
A Rebel's Guide to Eleanor Marx by Siobhan Brown
A Rebel's Guide to Rosa Luxemburg by Sally Campbell
A Rebel's Guide to Gramsci by Chris Bambery
A Rebel's Guide to Trotsky by Esme Choonara
A Rebel's Guide to Marx by Mike Gonzalez
A Rebel's Guide to Lenin by Ian Birchall
A Rebel's Guide to Malcolm X by Antony Hamilton
A Rebel's Guide to Martin Luther King by Yuri Prasad
Sexism and the System: A Rebel's Guide to Women's Liberation
    by Judith Orr
Available from Bookmarks, 1 Bloomsbury Street, London WC1B 3QE
bookmarksbookshop.co.uk | 020 7637 1848

★ INTRODUCTION

Walter Rodney was almost the same age as Malcolm X and Martin Luther King Jr when he was assassinated on 13 June 1980 in Guyana at the age of 38. Throughout his short life, he waged a relentless battle against the horrors of capitalism, for which he should be revered as one of the great black leaders of the last century.

Rodney is best known for his famous book *How Europe Underdeveloped Africa* which he wrote in Tanzania in 1972. Yet, his incredible journey and contributions to the struggle of the oppressed are largely unknown beyond Pan-African activist and academic circles. If some remember him as an influential Black Power advocate in Jamaica, few know about the time he spent in Africa. Fewer still remember the revolutionary struggle he led before his death in Guyana.

This short introduction is an overview of Rodney's life, activism and political thought, which aims to preserve and promote his legacy. Rodney's family and the Walter Rodney Foundation have already done important work in this respect. In recent years, they have republished Rodney's *Groundings with My Brothers*, *How Europe Underdeveloped Africa* and released his manuscript on the Russian Revolution. However, most biographies on Rodney are currently out of print. Readers unable to access academic libraries often cannot obtain Rupert Lewis's *Walter Rodney's Intellectual and Political Thought*. This book intends to encourage young black people to read about Rodney and fight for the ideas he stood for.

Scholars have attached various labels to Rodney's ideas and political identity. They have described him as a Pan-Africanist, a Black Nationalist or an anti-imperialist. Meanwhile, his most ardent supporters identify as 'Rodneyites'. Although there is some truth to all these descriptions, they fail to highlight that the mature Rodney aspired above all to be a Marxist. This point must be stressed, in particular, against those such as Manning Marable and Cedric Robinson who want to claim Rodney for the 'Black Radical' tradition, along with CLR James, WEB Du Bois and Richard Wright. The advocates of that tradition misconstrue Marxism as European in its outlook, and therefore incompatible with black liberation—Rodney never believed that. They suppose that black revolutionaries must outgrow Marxism to grasp the plight of black people against imperialism. Rodney's journey demonstrates the opposite: the more he developed his ideas, the greater he relied on Marxism to understand racism and organise for black liberation.

Yet Rodney's Marxist writing, speeches and activism extend beyond black liberation to outline key lessons for revolutionaries today. They teach us about the role of the working class as the gravedigger of capitalism. They also reflect on the debate about socialism from above versus socialism from below, and the role of radical intellectuals. Finally, they explain the Marxist view on race and class. Rodney does not have the final word on any of these topics. He died before he reached his full potential. But Rodney left behind a monumental body of work that strengthens our struggle against capitalism.

★ 1: THE EARLY YEARS

On 23 March 1942, during the Second World War, Pauline Rodney gave birth to her second son, Walter, in Georgetown, in what was then British Guyana. The 1939-1945 war, which ravaged Europe and weakened the British Empire, gave the colonised peoples of Africa, Asia and the Caribbean hope of winning their freedom. They organised mass movements against their colonial rulers through clubs, associations and political parties. In British Guyana, Pauline and her husband Edward joined the leading organisation of the nationalist movement, the People's Progressive Party (PPP), in the 1950s. She worked as a housewife and seamstress while he was an independent tailor who, in difficult times, sought work in large establishments. They were attracted to the PPP's anti-colonial rhetoric that promised a new society, where Guyanese workers would be wealthier and free. The Rodneys sent their elder children to distribute the PPP manifesto around the neighbourhood. Walter Rodney learnt at 11 years of age that those who owned wealthy houses often despised the PPP. He also realised that he wasn't welcome in their yards—he once had to run from a dog that someone let loose on him. Rodney would remember these leafleting sessions as his introduction to the class struggle.

Reminiscing upon his childhood in 1975, Rodney said he grew into Marxism with ease "because the PPP was the only mass party... and its leadership explicitly said, 'we are socialist'" (Walter Rodney, *The Making of an African Intellectual*, Africa World Press, New Jersey, 1990, pp6-7). He further praised the PPP for uniting Guyanese of African and Indian descent against the British. Such racial alliances were rare, given the British had historically divided both communities to better rule over them. Rodney's nostalgic recollection of the PPP's heyday echoed the overwhelming support Guyanese people gave the party in the 1950s. In 1953, the PPP won 75 percent of seats in the House Assembly elections and its leader, the Pro-Soviet Indian dentist Cheddi Jagan, became Prime Minister. But the PPP's rule only lasted 133 days, as the Cold War between the United States and the Soviet Union interfered in Guyanese politics. Under pressure from the USA, Britain sent troops to its colony to remove the PPP and allegedly stop the spread of 'communism'.

Despite its short rule, the PPP government managed to increase the number of educational scholarships available to young people. It wanted to prepare Guyana for independence by broadening the number of educated Guyanese. Rodney, who excelled at school, belonged to the only generation that benefited from the PPP's reform—he earned a scholarship to attend Queen's College, the most prestigious high school in the country. Most of his five siblings were not offered the same opportunities and dropped out of school when their parents could no longer afford tuition fees. In 1960, Rodney won another scholarship to study history at the University of the West Indies (UWI) in Kingston, Jamaica.

Rodney attended the UWI in the years leading to Jamaican independence from Britain in 1962. He witnessed the university embark on what he called a "nationalist pilgrimage", which broke ties with its colonial past. The Department of History stood at the forefront of this nationalist awakening. It was no longer exclusively preoccupied with teaching its students about European history and civilisation as it had done under colonialism. It now introduced classes on African history and the slave trade to help them better understand the factors that shaped Caribbean identity. It established Eric Williams' book *Capitalism and Slavery* and CLR James' *The Black Jacobins* as core readings on the curriculum. Few academics discussed these writings as examples of Marxist literature—instead, they served to arouse nationalist consciousness. West Indian students felt emotional when reading these books. Williams' writing revealed to them how the enslavement of their ancestors set in motion Western industrial development, while James' story of the Haitian Revolution of 1791 to 1804 gave them hope. They learnt that black people could resist their masters and win. These books encouraged Rodney to write an article on the cruelty of slavery entitled *The Negro Slave* and spend time in the campus library reading on pre-colonial African history.

Rodney's professors and peers adored him. He was a smart and friendly student. He captained the UWI debating team in his first year and made his reputation as a sharp mind and bold speaker. Rodney carried his speaking ability into student campaigns for the West Indies Federation—an unsuccessful regional project that aimed to merge former British colonies into a single independent state. But Rodney's enthusiasm for the UWI's nationalist pilgrimage faded. Even his most progressive nationalist teachers were complete philistines when it came to questions of class and socialism. The students were no better. Rodney lost his second presidential election to the West Indian Students' Union to a conservative candidate. His opponents accused him of being a dictator because he had travelled to Cuba. That criticism, however, did not discourage Rodney's fascination with Cuba. He had travelled to the island in 1960, a year after the victorious revolution, in which Fidel Castro and Che Guevara led a guerrilla war against the pro-American dictatorship. Fifteen years later, Rodney still remembered the pride and sense of freedom that the revolution gave the Cuban people. "The Cubans," he said, "were running and jumping, really living the revolution in a way that was completely outside of anything that one could read anywhere" (*The Making of an African Intellectual*, p17).

His journey to Moscow in his senior year also made a good impression on him. For the first time, he saw workers and peasants partaking in activities, such as aeroplane travel or ballet recitals that were reserved for the elite in Western countries. Rodney returned from his travels with literature. He took a keen interest in Lenin and wrote a paper on his leadership of the Russian Revolution of October 1917. Lenin's life experience showed Rodney that it was possible to be both a revolutionary organiser and an intellectual, unlike what his professors had told him. He now aspired to dedicate his radical intellect to strengthen the movements of the oppressed in the Global South. Rodney, however, would take his first major steps to become a Marxist thinker not in Jamaica but in London.

★ 2: THE FORMATION OF RODNEY'S MARXISM IN LONDON

Rodney faced racism when he arrived in London to pursue his doctorate in African history at the School of Oriental and African Studies (SOAS) in 1963. Although he had graduated with a first-class degree at UWI, SOAS almost forced him to take admission exams. If Rodney were a white English man, he wouldn't have had to justify himself. But he was a black man from the colonies and therefore British society saw him as inferior. Yet he felt privileged compared to his friends and his older brother who had migrated to England to seek work—they faced the brunt of job and housing discrimination. The resistance of black people in Britain to racism fascinated Rodney. He spent much of his free time speaking at Hyde Park Corner where West Indians gathered to discuss politics. He talked about racism, Caribbean politics, apartheid and Zimbabwean independence. Rodney was happy to reunite with his girlfriend Patricia, who had left Guyana for Britain to work as a nurse. They had started dating in the summer before Rodney went to university in Jamaica and maintained a long-distance relationship until he arrived in London. Having reunited, the couple deepened their affection for one another and married in 1965.

In England, Rodney aimed to develop his engagement with Marxism in order to relate to the black working class. SOAS, however, proved unable to help him with such a task. "There was nobody," he lamented, "who could be remotely termed a Marxist" (*The Making of An African Intellectual*, p27). Rodney thought that SOAS, which was founded in 1916 to train British colonial administrators, now educated Africans to serve the interests of Europe. He despised his curriculum and his pretentious professors entrenched in bourgeois ideology. For example, one of his lecturers, the renowned historian John D Fage, argued that the slave trade had benefited West African development, and did no harm to the region's demographics and economy. Rodney challenged Fage's defence of the slave trade in his thesis *A History of the Upper Guinea Coast 1545-1800*. Although he thought his dissertation showed no strong Marxist scholarship, it was nonetheless the work of a people's historian. Rodney portrayed pre-colonial West Africa as innovative and culturally refined and countered the narrative of Western scholars that depicted it as primitive. He exposed how European powers disrupted the lives of African people and their societies through the slave trade. Rodney sought to develop this theme in his later work "to upset ... the deans of African history in London" (*The Making of An African Intellectual*, p36).

The British Marxist left of the time made a poor impression on Rodney. He was repelled by the sectarianism of the Communist Party and the different, smaller Trotskyist groups that he came across. They seemed to him more interested in debating amongst themselves than organising workers and defending migrants. He found them old, inarticulate and unprepared. Rodney, moreover, accused the British left of neglecting the fight against racism. He resented the paternalism, the silent and sometimes open racism he encountered from some of them. Rodney was not the first black activist to be frustrated with the British left. Before him, Claudia Jones, the founder of the Notting Hill Carnival and a member of the Communist Party, had criticised her own party for marginalising anti-racism in the 1950s. But Rodney found solace in a Marxist study group taught by CLR James and his wife Selma. From 1963 to 1966, he and a handful of radical West Indian students visited James' home in North West London on Friday evenings.

Rodney saw in CLR James qualities that he admired. James never went to university, yet he was a brilliant Trinidadian Marxist scholar, a prolific writer and a powerful orator. As a black Bolshevik, he placed the liberation of Africans and colonised peoples at the core of his politics. In his earlier Trotskyist days, James led campaigns against Mussolini's invasion of Ethiopia before writing his path-breaking Marxist history of the Haitian Revolution, *The Black Jacobins*, in 1938. Although James had long broken with Trotskyism when Rodney met him in the 1960s, he was still in a class of his own. He had recently returned from Trinidad and Tobago after opposing the despotism of his old friend, Prime Minister Eric Williams, by resigning as editor of his party's newspaper. James taught Rodney about Marx's theory of historical change and the Russian Revolution. They read classics such as Marx's *The 18th Brumaire of Louis Bonaparte* and Lenin's *What Is to Be Done*.

From listening to James, Rodney learnt about the revolutionary potential of the working class through its past and present militancy in Europe and abroad. He discovered that exploitation gave workers immense power, as the capitalist relied on their labour-power to make profits—if workers engaged in mass strikes, they could bring the capitalist system to a halt. Rodney also wrote a paper on Marxism and democracy to show what the workers must do to the state in a revolution. Years later, he wrote about the lessons of the Russian Revolution: "The workers could not simply take over a bourgeois parliament and consider the revolution achieved...the bourgeois state had to be destroyed and replaced by institutions which sprang from the working masses" (Walter Rodney, *The Russian Revolution: A View From The Third World*, Verso, 2018, p108). That's how well he understood the key concepts of Lenin's *State and Revolution*.

Rodney's understanding of Marxism was also shaped by a world in which the Communist parties of the Soviet Union, China and Cuba had conquered state-power and challenged Western imperialism. That most Third World nationalist movements and regimes in the 1960s identified with socialism and sometimes called themselves Marxist was no coincidence. They received material and logistical support from the Soviet Union, which hoped to find allies in the Cold War against the United States. Moreover, they looked to the Chinese (1949) and Cuban (1959) revolutions because they appeared to offer a new path to socialism that suited the interest of underdeveloped countries that had a large peasantry and a small working class. The idea that guerrilla struggle in the countryside was essential to achieve national liberation became central to Third World nationalist 'Marxism'.

Many on the European left, who opposed the Soviet Union's bureaucratic oppression of workers and peasants, came to see Mao's China and Castro's Cuba as favourable socialist alternatives. Rodney's mentor CLR James, for instance, supported the workers' Hungarian Revolution of 1956 against the Soviet Union and advocated for a proletarian revolution in the advanced Western capitalist countries. But he also saw the Cuban Revolution and its strategy of guerrilla warfare as a model for Third World revolutions (see CLR James, 'The Gathering Forces', 1967 unless otherwise stated all articles referred to are available at marxists.org). Rodney would display a similar ambivalence towards revolutionary strategy as Third World guerrilla intellectuals such as Che Guevara, Frantz Fanon and Amílcar Cabral, influenced him as much as Marx and Lenin. While he acknowledged the centrality of strikes and workers' struggles in his later writings on the Russian Revolution, he also believed that guerrilla warfare presented a viable approach to revolutions in the Global South.

Rodney, however, failed to understand why the strategy of guerrilla warfare that the Third World revolutions adopted was incompatible with Marxism, which emphasised revolution through working class self-activity. As guerrilla warfare involved shifting the struggle from the town to the countryside, Third World intellectuals claimed the agent of the revolution was not the urban working class but the peasantry led by commanders from the urban middle class. They had thus revised Marxism and removed it from its proletarian base.

Che Guevara saw the working class in underdeveloped countries as a weak and impotent force, while Fanon even claimed it as an obstacle to national liberation because workers benefited from colonialism. The Guinean leader Amílcar Cabral, who directed the guerrilla war against Portugal in Guinea-Bissau with unparalleled success in Africa, had initially attempted to organise the small working class in Bissau. However, he turned to guerrilla struggle after the Portuguese massacre of 50 dockworkers in 1959. Che Guevara continued to pay lip service to the international proletarian revolution and affiliate with Marxism despite his revisions. He wrote: "The peasant class of Latin America, basing itself on the ideology of the working class whose great thinkers discovered the social laws governing us, will provide the great liberating army of the future" (Che Guevara, 'Cuba: Historical Exception or Vanguard in the Anticolonial Struggle', 1961).

Guevara forgot that the great thinkers—Marx, Trotsky and Lenin—had argued that the essence of a socialist revolution lies in the self-emancipation of the working class, whereby "the proletariat becomes the subject of history, not the object" (see Tony Cliff, *Deflected Permanent Revolution*, 1963). In the absence of the proletariat, the guerrilla wars of the Third World led not to socialism but to bureaucratic one-party regimes that resembled the Soviet Union. The seeds of this failure were obvious in the contradiction in aims within the guerrilla army—the elitist middle-class commanders wanted to rule, while the peasants wanted land. As a result, the middle class mobilised the peasantry to give itself state power, and then exploited and oppressed the masses to bring the nation out of underdevelopment.

Despite its flaws, guerrilla warfare had nonetheless inflicted serious defeats to Western imperialism in Africa, Asia and Latin America. By the mid-1960s, it had become the main form of anti-colonial resistance in Portuguese-speaking and southern Africa. That explains why Rodney, throughout his life, saw this strategy as a high form of politics, convinced that it forced revolutionaries to educate and mobilise the masses. He believed in the redemptive qualities of revolutionary violence that Fanon discussed in his book on anti-colonial struggles, *The Wretched of the Earth* Fanon argued that this violence freed the colonised from their inferiority complex and transformed them into proud independent people. Rodney especially saw this transformation occur in the guerrilla liberation movements against Portuguese colonialism in Mozambique, Angola and Guinea-Bissau. He felt attached to them, as he had witnessed Portuguese dictator Salazar's repressive fascism when he was conducting his PhD research in Lisbon.

The national liberation movements in the Global South informed Rodney's ideas on the role of revolutionary intellectuals in the struggle. Rodney was particularly impressed with Amílcar Cabral. He admired that Cabral had thoroughly analysed the formation of the various classes in his country and based his anti-colonial mobilisation strategy upon the sensitivities of each class towards the colonial state. In his analysis of Guinean society in 1964, Cabral had found that the educated middle class, which he belonged to, could become an elitist and greedy caste that would compromise with the old colonial power to enrich itself (Amílcar Cabral, *Revolution in Guinea*, 1964). However, he idealistically maintained that this middle class also had the potential to lead the anti-colonial struggle only if it committed "class suicide" to resurrect itself as revolutionary cadres "identified with the deepest aspirations of the people to which they belong" (Amílcar Cabral, 'Weapon of Theory', 1966). Rodney nevertheless took from Cabral the idea that revolutionary intellectuals must understand the historical reality they seek to transform. They must do away with their elitism, learn from the people and grasp their needs to influence the struggle.

On 5 July 1966, the day Patricia gave birth to their son Shaka, Rodney earned his PhD in African history. He then moved with his family to Tanzania to teach history for one year and meet the Mozambican and Angolan freedom fighters stationed there. But Rodney forged his reputation as a revolutionary when he relocated to Jamaica to lecture at the University of the West Indies (UWI) in January 1968.

★ 3: FIGHTING FOR BLACK POWER IN JAMAICA (1968)

On the morning of 16 October 1968, 900 students gathered at the UWI campus and began marching to Kingston. They were angered by the Jamaican government's decision to expel their beloved professor Walter Rodney from the island. They did not get far before the police tear-gassed and beat them into retreat. But the students returned more determined that afternoon. Now they had thousands of Rastafarians, working class and unemployed youths in their ranks. When they invaded Kingston, they did what the young people of Paris, Prague and the black neighbourhoods of America had done that spring and summer of 1968. In Jamaica, they set fire to 15 buses and looted American and Canadian companies, chanting "Black Power" until dawn.

In part, Rodney's Black Power advocacy had inspired Jamaica's youth. However, the real significance of the 'Rodney riots' went beyond demands for his reinstatement. It lay in the poverty and political exclusion of Jamaicans and the rise of black consciousness among the youth. The young protesters, like most Jamaicans, descended from the thousands of African slaves that British colonialism had transported to be exploited on the sugar cane plantations of Jamaica for over two centuries. Their ancestors resisted slavery, but never managed to take control of the island's wealth from their masters. In the century after emancipation in 1838 many of them became wage-labourers on the declining British sugar estates, while others became poor peasants. The luckier ones later found work on the docks and in the Western-owned banana and bauxite industries of the 20th century. These workers unleashed a wave of strikes and protests against colonialism in response to the suffering caused by the Great Depression of the 1930s. But the great labour unrest of the 1930s, which also swept the entire British West Indies, sadly ended in defeat.

The unrest nevertheless forced Britain to open its administration to the tiny number of educated Jamaicans, who inherited state-power after independence in 1962. The new rulers prospered under the Jamaican Labour Party (JLP) government, through the substantial foreign investment they received from Western companies. They were white, brown, Lebanese and Chinese but had very few blacks among their ranks—a glaring disparity given that 90 percent of Jamaican citizens were the descendants of African slaves. Thus, freedom from Britain meant nothing for most Jamaicans. Rural poverty and unemployment on the decaying estates forced many to migrate to Kingston, often to join the ranks of an estimated 150,000 slum dwellers.

In the 1950s and 1960s, Black Nationalism gave expression to the anger of poor black youths at the political elite and the multinationals. The radical labour movement of the 1930s had been defeated. The JLP and its rival, the People's National Party (PNP), had co-opted the trade unions and turned them into electoral machines. The corruption of the trade unions and the absence of alternative organisational models partly explain the adventurism and tendency to engage in conspiratorial plots that characterised some of Jamaica's Black Nationalist movements. In 1960, for instance, the Jamaican authorities and the CIA uncovered the plot of an Afrocentric evangelical sect, led by Rev Claudius Henry, to overthrow the Jamaican Government. Three years after the Henry Rebellion, the state attacked a much larger black Christian movement, the Rastafarians.

Originating in the 1930s as reaction to British rule, under the influence of Protestant religious leaders who preached African pride and political figures such as Marcus Garvey who advocated that black people should go 'Back to Africa', by the 1960s, thousands of black youth had converted to Rastafarianism and adopted a countercultural lifestyle that ranged from ganja smoking and dreadlock growing, to squatting and small-scale farming. Squatting made them the subject of evictions and police brutality. In 1963, six Rastafarians attacked a petrol station on the Coral Gardens property that resulted in the killing of nine people, including two policemen. The assault was an act of revenge against the landlords and the government's attempts to evict squatters to repurpose the land for tourism. The police and the army retaliated by arresting 150 innocent Rastafarians.

Rastafarianism was a threat to the ruling class because it criticised its multiracial composition and its lavish Western lifestyle. Rastafarianism rested upon the belief that black people were the captives of Babylon, an evil system of corruption and oppression that Western civilisation had created, which the Jamaican elite upheld. It proclaimed that black people could only find salvation by returning "home" to Africa—which they called "Zion", the promised land. For many Rastafarians, the notion of repatriation was less about an actual return to Africa than a return at the level of consciousness, which included the restitution of African pride and the adoption of a way of life that was antagonistic to Western culture. The Rastafarians preached love, self-respect and freedom from the shackles of mental and physical slavery for those of African descent who suffered from the legacies of slavery and colonisation. They offered black youths an ideological and spiritual framework that helped them understand their suffering and revolt against it.

The elite sometimes resorted to peaceful means when trying to accommodate the agitation around black consciousness. In 1964, the JLP repatriated the corpse of Marcus Garvey and honoured him as a national hero. The elite knew that Garvey inspired many Jamaicans who valued their African heritage. In 1914, while he still lived in Jamaica, Garvey had established the Universal Negro Improvement Association (UNIA)—the largest ever Black Nationalist organisation—which he then set up in Harlem, New York when he moved there in 1916. The UNIA exerted a strong influence on the emergence of Black Nationalism in the United States but as an organisation it declined after the American Government imprisoned and deported Garvey to Jamaica in 1927. Thirteen years later, Garvey died a poor and forgotten man in London. But Rastafarians remembered him as a martyr and celebrated his legacy.

In 1966, the JLP invited Emperor Haile Selassie of Ethiopia, whom the Rastafarians worshipped as the Messiah of black people and the incarnation of God.

The Rastafarians revered Ethiopia because it was never colonised by Europe—it symbolised a free and independent Africa. They furthermore regarded the 1500-year-old Ethiopian Coptic Church as the custodian of an authentic Christianity that remained uncorrupted by Western influences. So, when news of the emperor's visit spread across the island, crowds rushed to greet Selassie on the tarmac, breaking through all security barriers. Some believe the unofficial parades celebrating Selassie's arrival were even bigger than those on Independence Day. Whether this was true or not, the visit increased the legitimacy and following of the Rastafari. The ruling class, however, feared that Black Nationalism was proving too difficult to control. The growing influence of the American Black Power movement in Jamaica added to their panic.

In 1968, the JLP banned all Black Power literature from the USA, fearful of the extent to which the ideas of the Black Panthers, the Nation of Islam and Malcolm X were inspiring Jamaican students and academics. It resented the formation of a militant alliance between radical black intellectuals and the masses. That year, the Jamaican ruling party also monitored the activities of a 26-year-old lecturer named Walter Rodney who had arrived on the island in January. What did Rodney do to get expelled in October? And how had he won the hearts and minds of the masses during his short stay on the island?

★ 4: GROUNDING WITH MY BROTHERS (1968)

Eight months prior to his banning from Jamaica, Rodney was appointed lecturer in African history at the UWI. His students admired his kindness and modesty. Rodney was different from the academics that returned from London with dandy shirts and a fake British accent. Rodney wore dashikis—a West African form of dress—an Afro haircut and spoke English with a Guyanese twang, yet he had also earned a PhD. Unlike his ivory-tower colleagues, Rodney refused to live on the UWI campus and settled in West Kingston to be closer to the poor and oppressed. He believed the role of the radical intellectual was to help the masses win their struggles and he intended to use his knowledge for that purpose.

People respected Rodney for his public lectures on Black Power at the students' union. He was a talented speaker who attracted dozens of listeners on campus. After one of his speeches, Rodney made friends with three Rastafarians who then connected him to grassroots activist circles and the masses. One of them, Jerry Small, had turned his back on his middle-class upbringing to live among the poor. He invited Rodney to the groundings—the informal religious gathering that Rastafarians organised in the shantytowns of Kingston.

Rodney enjoyed listening to the activists he met at those meetings. Among them, the Rev Claudius Henry left a big impression on him. The reverend had served a six-year prison sentence for conspiring to overthrow the government in 1960. Rodney visited Henry's Pan-African church and was struck by what he saw. He wrote:

In Kemp's Hill, in the middle of a most depressed area, which is the Prime Minister's constituency, Rev Henry has gathered together a number of black brothers and sisters, and they have turned themselves into an independent black economic community. In less than a year they built themselves an attractive church and several dwelling houses, all of concrete for they make the concrete blocks (Quoted in Rupert Lewis, *Walter Rodney: 1968 Revisited*, UWI Press, 1998).

This passage highlighted Rodney's support for the attempts of ordinary working people to manage their own affairs when abandoned by the state. Yet, he thought that the black masses could achieve more than build a community—they could rule the island. He was ready to speak to them about Black Power and its relevance to Jamaica and the Caribbean.

According to Rodney's friend Robert Hill, leaflets were never distributed to promote the groundings. Yet two to three hundred people came to hear Rodney speak on African history and Jamaican politics around a campfire on Sunday mornings. The Labour Party, which governed the island, saw Rodney as a Guyanese troublemaker and spied on him. Rodney did not join or build any organisation. He was just an intellectual interacting with the masses, yet the Jamaican ruling class felt threatened by his message of Black Power. Rodney spoke of Black Power as an ideology and movement against the oppression of black people by whites under capitalism. He defined Black Power in the West Indies as: "(1) The break with imperialism, which is historically white racist; (2) the assumption of power by the black masses in the islands; (3) the cultural reconstruction of society in the image of blacks" (Walter Rodney, *The Groundings with my Brothers*, Bogle L'Ouverture Publications, London, 1969, p38). Although Rodney viewed Black Power as a universal call for self-determination, he thought its relevance to the West Indies differed from that in America. In the United States, the programme of most radical black leaders reflected the position of an African American racial minority who faced employment and housing discrimination and police brutality from mainly white police officers. The principal theoretician of Black Power, Stokely Carmichael (later known as Kwame Ture) argued for blacks in the US to take political and economic control of their communities away from the police and the state. Carmichael's views would later radicalise and he would join the Black Panthers, who advocated a socialist revolution in 1968.

Unlike in America, African descendants were the majority in most of the ex-British West Indies and suffered oppression from both blacks and other non-white peoples. So Rodney theorised Black Power in a more radical way than Carmichael, to challenge the domination of what he called the "white imperialist system" (*Groundings*, p41). This referred to the collusion between the local black elite and the Western multinational companies that exploited workers and robbed the Caribbean of its raw materials. Rodney also anchored his Black Power in internationalism by linking the struggles of Jamaicans to liberation movements in the Global South fighting colonialism and imperialism. Moreover, he argued that West Indian Black Power concerned Indians and Africans alike. In his homeland, Guyanese Indians outnumbered Africans and they made up half of the population of Trinidad and Tobago. Both peoples, he maintained, shared a history of bondage and oppression at the hands of imperialism. The British Empire had bought Africans as slaves, and then shipped Indians as indentured labour. Now both communities endured poverty and saw power denied to them.

In Jamaica, Rodney criticised the ruling class for flaunting the myth of a harmonious multiracial Jamaican society. He despised its national motto—"Out of Many, One People"—for obscuring the fact that a small multiracial elite ruled over an African majority. For Rodney, the elite feared above all the prospect of Jamaicans organising politically around their African identity. Therefore, many of his speeches emphasised the need for blacks to reconnect with their African heritage. Rodney aspired to dismantle the inferiority complex that slavery, colonialism and racism instilled among blacks by representing Africa as primitive and uncivilised. He told black students in San Francisco in 1968: "We are the only group in the world who deny ourselves preferring to be known as Negros... To know ourselves we must learn about African history" (*Groundings*, p33). Rodney had a similar message for his Jamaican audience. At the groundings, he spoke at length on the great empires of Ethiopia, Kush and Benin.

The empirical evidence he presented in his lectures strengthened the religious claims that Rastafarians held on the grandeur of ancient African civilisations. The Rastafarians nicknamed him 'the African doctor' because of his knowledge of African history.

Although Rodney argued that history was a crucial weapon for mobilising black people, he thought its importance was secondary to the tactics and strategy of revolution. What was the correct revolutionary strategy for Jamaica? Rodney grappled with this question that weighed so heavily on his mind. He had reservations on whether the Jamaican masses were willing to support armed struggle against their ruling class. "I doubt whether the situation is explosive," he wrote in a letter to his wife. While Rodney admired Che Guevara's teaching on guerrilla warfare, he knew that this strategy could not be blindly applied to the Jamaican context, even though it had proved successful in many parts of the Global South. Guevara himself had warned revolutionaries about the impossibility of waging an effective guerrilla war without securing the support of the masses of workers and peasants.

Instead, Rodney took from Guevara's life experience the need to agitate for more concrete action. "All that matters," he wrote, "is the question of action: determined, informed and scientific action against imperialism and its cohorts" (Rupert Lewis, *Walter Rodney's Intellectual and Political Thought*, UWI Press, 1998, pIII). Where did theory fit in this picture? Rodney seldom mentioned his affinity with Marxism in his speeches at the groundings. Perhaps, he did not want to alienate the Rastafarians around him who were hostile to socialism. Rodney did celebrate the emergence of a rank-and-file workers' movement that staged strikes without the support of the state co-opted unions. Yet the workers figured as only one of the revolutionary classes that he identified. He did not view their struggles against capital in Jamaica as central to the revolution. Instead he placed most of his revolutionary faith in the unemployed black youth.

In one of the lectures he gave at Montreal's Black Writers Conference in October 1968, Rodney spoke with passion about the Jamaican youth's growing readiness to fight: "Throughout the country, black youth are becoming aware of the possibilities of unleashing armed struggle in their own interest. For those who have eyes to see, there is already evidence of the beginning of resistance to the violence of our oppressors" (*Groundings*, pp23-24). The Jamaican government barred Rodney from entering Jamaica upon his return from the conference. Unfortunately, the Rodney Riots that ensued failed to reinstate him as the police beat the protesters into retreat and occupied the UWI campus for several days. While the riots appeared as a moment of unity between middle-class students, the unemployed and working class youths, they failed to produce a long-lasting mass movement in Jamaica. The sheer brutality of the government's repression ultimately demoralised the Jamaican masses.

Caribbean Black Power instead peaked in 1970 with the Trinidadian revolution that almost overthrew President Eric Williams. Although they were defeated, the Trinidadian workers proved to be the locus of power—their strikes paralysed the economy and fuelled the anti-government protests. Rodney did not foresee this potential for working class struggle when discussing

Black Power in the Caribbean. Meanwhile, Jamaican Black Nationalism was dragged into the party rivalry between the JLP and the People's National Party, cynically described as "gun politics". Both parties financed gangs to suppress rival supporters and to win swing constituencies. By the 1980s, the turf wars had divided and absorbed the once-radical ghetto youths. Contrary to what Rodney believed at the time, the youths did not have the coherence and the power to lead the struggle.

Despite the failure of Black Power, Rodney's activism in Jamaica is still remembered today in reggae songs and activist circles. At only 26 years of age, Rodney had galvanised the oppressed masses and frightened the political establishment. News of his exploits in Jamaica reached two Afro-Guyanese activists, Jessica and Eric Huntley, who owned a radical bookshop in London. In 1969, they met Rodney and published his speeches on Black Power under the title *The Groundings With My Brothers*. In his pamphlet, Rodney asserted that the Jamaican government was wrong to believe that his expulsion from the island would stifle the masses. "This act," he concluded, "will not delay its day of judgment" (*Groundings*, p74). His faith in the self-activity of the masses would remain with him throughout the rest of his life.

★5: TANZANIA, THE MECCA OF AFRICAN LIBERATION (1969-1974)

Karim Hirji, a Tanzanian student, was in a good mood when he went to bed on 10 July 1969. That evening he had heard the most impressive lecture of his life at the University of Dar es Salaam. The lecture was on the Cuban Revolution and its relevance to Africa. Back in his dorm, he praised the speaker in his diary: "One could almost feel the strong conviction and deep emotions from which he spoke" (Karim Hirji, *The Enduring Relevance of Walter Rodney's How Europe Underdeveloped Africa*, Mkuki Na Nyota, Dar es Salaam, 2017). The man he admired and later befriended was Dr Walter Rodney.

After being banned from Jamaica, Rodney settled with his family in Tanzania to teach history and political science at the University of Dar es Salaam from 1969 to 1974. He reconnected with the socialist students he had met during his first stay in 1966. In those days, Rodney helped them establish the University Students African Revolutionary Front (USARF). He ran their Marxist workshops and attended their anti-imperialist protests and talks. His connections brought the likes of CLR James,

Stokely Carmichael and Guyanese politician Cheddi Jagan to speak on USARF platforms. Upon his return in 1969, Rodney was pleased to see that the USARF had gained new members. Karim Hirji was one of them. He got Rodney to write the first article for the group's magazine *Cheche* on African labour (*Cheche* took its name from Lenin's newspaper *Iskra*. Both words mean 'spark'). Rodney thus continued agitating for socialism on campus as he had done in Jamaica. But the political climate was now more favourable for him, as Tanzania was the mecca of African liberation.

Tanzania offered hope to Rodney and many radical black intellectuals. They believed the African diaspora's fight for freedom and equality relied on the success of anti-imperialist movements in Africa. Tanzania's first president Julius Nyerere and his party, the Tanganyika African Nation Union (TANU) opposed imperialism as few independent African states did. Nyerere gave diplomatic and material support to every national liberation movement in southern Africa. He opened offices for the Liberation Front of Mozambique (FRELIMO) and built military bases for them. He established training camps for the paramilitary wing of Nelson Mandela's African National Congress, uMkhonto we Sizwe, to help it fight the apartheid regime in South Africa. Living in Tanzania enabled Rodney to deepen his understanding of guerrilla warfare and international solidarity. FRELIMO fighters taught him how to shoot a rifle when he visited their camps. He also met with delegations from Vietnam, then involved in the war against the United States, and organised solidarity protests with the Vietnamese on campus.

When Rodney first visited Tanzania in 1966, he witnessed Nyerere publish his programme for socialism and self-reliance, the Arusha Declaration. The president had turned his African socialist philosophy known as Ujamaa—familyhood—into a policy of nationalisation of foreign companies and land reform. He aspired to increase food production through the creation of Ujamaa villages based on collective farming. Africans no longer had to rely on volatile cash crops and aid from advanced capitalist nations to make a living. Nyerere was confident that his plan suited the interest of the peasant majority. But he had yet to convince the minuscule educated elite, made up of students and state officials, to help the peasants. Back in 1964, some elitist students had shown Nyerere their disdain for work in the countryside when they protested against compulsory national service. Afterwards, Nyerere vowed to turn the university into a battleground for his progressive ideas.

By 1970, Rodney stood at the heart of the debates concerning African underdevelopment that occurred almost every night at the university. In the packed auditorium, Rodney debated a TANU cabinet minister on Tanzania's economic direction. He also debated the renowned Kenyan political science professor, Ali Mazuri, on why Africa should be socialist, not capitalist. His ideas, however, did not always please Nyerere. The president replied with anger to an article Rodney published in TANU's newspaper, which argued that African leaders who served Western capitalism deserved to be overthrown by the people. Nyerere disagreed and accused him of preaching violence to young people. The regime set limits on how left-wing students and academics could be. A few months later, it banned the USARF for promoting "foreign ideology" (Hirji, p95).

The ban did not change Rodney's respect for Nyerere, nor did it discourage him from sharing his radical Marxist ideas with students. He taught a graduate course on the Russian Revolution to show his African students that they could draw lessons for their own struggle from October 1917. He made parallels between present-day Tanzania and Tsarist Russia, which both had a large peasantry and a small working class. Rodney praised the Russian Revolution as the first break with capitalism, transforming the once mainly agrarian country into an industrial power in its aftermath. Bourgeois historians, he argued, sought to discredit October 1917 because it represented the victory of organised workers allied with peasants over their class.

Rodney had begun a monograph on the Russian Revolution in 1971, but he never finished it because he had more urgent matters at hand. He wanted to use Marxist theory to address the issue of African underdevelopment.

★ 6: HOW EUROPE UNDER- DEVELOPED AFRICA

Rodney's involvement in debates concerning African underdevelopment in Tanzania inspired him to write his most influential book, *How Europe Underdeveloped Africa*. He was concerned that most African nations had not broken ties with the old colonial powers in the decade after colonialism. They had achieved political independence, but their economies remained in the hands of European and American companies. They remained poor and reliant on foreign aid because the Western ruling class stole their natural wealth (land, oil etc) for its benefit, with help from the African leaders who served them. Yet, many African intellectuals still believed that trade deals, loans and investment from advanced capitalist countries would benefit African development. Rodney sought to convince them to the contrary.

His book, published in 1972, revealed that European intervention in Africa, through the slave trade and colonialism, stifled African development. It told how the European ruling class robbed Africa of its wealth, which contributed to Europe's prosperity and industrial growth. Rodney examined Africa's relationship with Europe from 1500 to 1960 to elucidate the present. He opened the preface with his message for the future: "African development is only possible on the basis of a radical break with the international capitalist system," which had underdeveloped Africa for centuries (Walter Rodney, *How Europe Underdeveloped Africa*, Pambazuka Press, Cape Town 2012, Pxi).

Rodney's skilful use of Marx's historical method in his book uprooted Africa from the colonial myths surrounding its past. In chapter one, Rodney dismantled the racist idea that Africa stood outside progress by defining development as a universal and multifaceted process. As Marx and Engels did before him, he understood development as being rooted in how human beings cooperate to provide the necessities of life out of nature. He explained that when people found better ways to produce wealth by working together, they developed new forms of cooperation, new ideas and changed the form of their society. Rodney showed a sophisticated understanding of development, arguing that it did not unfold as a linear process but rather was uneven across continents and regions, as sometimes the people who defended old forms of cooperation and ideas stopped those attempting to modernise production, delaying societal change for years to come.

Rodney dedicated the second chapter to portraying Africa's development before Europeans arrived in the 1500s. Far from being outside of progress, Africa displayed formidable advances in agriculture, science and art. Most societies at the time were small classless ones with low levels of production, where people had equal access to land and evenly shared resources. Africa, however, developed more hierarchical societies that resembled

Europe's feudal states in places like Ethiopia, Egypt and Zimbabwe. In these unequal societies, a ruling class owned the land and appropriated the surplus created by the exploited peasants. Rodney argued that underdevelopment was never the absence of development. It was not inherent to Africa and its people, but the historical consequence of capitalist expansion and imperialism.

By the 16th century, Europe developed at a faster pace than Africa and the rest of the world, transitioning from feudalism to capitalism. Rodney argued that European powers demonstrated their superiority in maritime and armaments technology. They opened West Africa for trade with their ships and canons and transformed it into a supplier of slaves for their plantations in America and the Caribbean. In the third and fourth chapters, Rodney explored the consequences of the transatlantic slave trade on African development by engaging in the debate concerning the number of African captives. He opposed Philip Curtin's tally that counted only 10 million enslaved from 1500 to 1870. "Because it is a low figure it is already being used by European scholars who are apologists for the capitalist system and its long record of brutality" (HEUA, p96). Rodney explained that Curtin's toll failed to measure the whole tragedy because it only relied on records of slaves' arrivals in America. The number of victims went far beyond 10 million, as some captives were smuggled and millions more never left Africa. They died in the wars fought over slaves and more captives perished during the long journeys from the interior of Africa to the coast as well as the so-called 'Middle Passage', the journey across the Atlantic.

After he established the horrific magnitude of the slave

trade, Rodney explained how it underdeveloped Africa. He showed that the trade stunted Africa's demographic growth. As European powers kidnapped able young men and women, Africa lost those of childbearing age who performed the most arduous tasks on the land. With fewer people at hand, many African societies struggled to harness nature and develop. Moreover, Rodney argued that Europe's demand for slaves made slave raiding and wars commonplace in West Africa. Societies that had hitherto coexisted in peace now turned on each other to acquire more slaves. Violence instilled fear and insecurity among Africans. It disrupted the organisation of agriculture, mining and commerce that they had established over centuries. It destroyed crops and artisanal trade, turning farmers into soldiers, and soldiers into slaves. This disruption of farming and trade even impeded the development of African regions that were not involved in the slave trade.

While the slave trade stalled and reversed African development, it contributed to Europe's capitalist development. Rodney demonstrated that the slave trade generated enormous profits for the Portuguese, British and French empires, making fortunes for countless bourgeois merchants and plantation owners. Its wealth and magnitude gave rise to the infamous ports of Bristol, Liverpool, Nantes and Bordeaux. He explained how the profits and goods accrued from the exploitation of African slaves in the New World fuelled Britain's Industrial Revolution. A century ago, Karl Marx had made the same point when he wrote, "Without slavery there would be no cotton, without cotton there would be no modern industry" (Karl Marx & Friedrich Engels,

Collected Works, Vol.38, International Publishers, New York, 1846/1982, pp95-106). At the end of chapter four, Rodney explained how colonialism emerged out of the imperialist stage of capitalism in the late 19th century. Rivalries between European capitalist firms assumed the form of a competition between nation-states for control over the world's markets, natural resources and trade routes. Africa, which had been weakened from centuries of slave trading, fell victim to Europe's violent colonial conquest. European ruling classes justified this conquest with racist ideology, as they claimed to be civilising savage people by converting them to Christianity. Thus, by 1900, they had divided the entire African continent into colonies.

In the fifth chapter, Rodney analysed colonialism (1885-1960) as a cruel and exploitative system, whereby the European bourgeoisie extracted wealth from African workers and peasants. He assessed the oppression and suffering of African workers at the hands of the colonial state. The state ensured that Africans often worked under forced labour, while their European counterparts could freely sell their labour. Even those Africans who were able to choose their employer received miserable wages for endless hours of work. Colonial rule was even worse for the African peasant. Rodney showed how the colonial state confiscated their land through severe taxation, evictions and warfare. It forced some peasants to abandon food production for export crops that were sold cheap. Moreover, peasants suffered at the hands of trading companies and their middlemen who offered miserable prices. Rodney, however, did not simply illustrate the horrors of colonialism. He provided case studies of multinational companies, like Unilever, and the enormous profits they acquired from robbing Africans. Moreover, he described how Africa's contribution to capitalism went beyond monetary returns. Its raw materials supported Europe's advancement in electronics, metallurgy and chemistry and other industries, which stood at the centre of Europe's capitalist development in the 20th century.

In the final chapter, Rodney attacked the racist idea that colonialism had benefits for Africans because the colonisers built railroads, schools and hospitals. All the roads and railways, he said, went from the plantations and mines to the coast to ship raw materials to Europe, never to encourage trade between different regions of Africa. The infrastructure that colonialists built served to entrench Africa's unfavourable position in the world economy, as a precarious supplier of raw materials and a free market for European finished products. The colonialists had no interest in providing health care and education to Africans. Rodney established the grim tally of five centuries of Portuguese colonisation: "The Portuguese had not managed to train a single African doctor in Mozambique, and the life expectancy in Eastern Angola was less than thirty years" (*HEUA*, p206).

Rodney's historical account received support from Tanzania's radical socialist minister A M Babu who clarified Africa's present predicament in the postscript. "Foreign investment," the minister wrote, "is the cause, and not a solution, to our economic backwardness" (*HEUA*, p284). Investment went into projects designed to exploit African labour and raw materials for the benefit of the Western ruling class, never into healthcare and education. At best, foreign investment made fortunes for the few African leaders and businessmen who partnered with Western states and multinationals. But it failed to uplift the masses from poverty. Babu and Rodney advocated a revolutionary path to development, aimed at breaking Africa's dependence on imperialist powers and empowering the workers and peasants. What would that path look like? Initially, Rodney thought that Nyerere's socialism offered an answer to that question.

★ 7: RODNEY AND UJAMAA: SOCIALISM FROM ABOVE OR BELOW

Rodney's friends remembered the parties that he and Patricia hosted at their house in Dar es Salaam. When Rodney wasn't working, there was always someone visiting the couple to discuss politics or play dominoes. Patricia described her husband as a good family man; he did house chores and cooked—he loved making Chinese food. Patricia gave birth to their daughters Kanini in 1969 and Asha in 1971. Rodney enjoyed spending time and playing with his kids. When he visited Ujamaa villages near Dodoma in 1970 with the USARF and the TANU youth league, he brought his son Shaka along. Rodney lodged there for weeks and worked on installations for farming. He relished every opportunity to meet peasants and learn about Tanzanian socialism.

Rodney grew fascinated with Ujamaa. He saw it as a radical initiative to eradicate poverty in the countryside. By 1973, TANU had moved 15 percent of the peasantry from isolated homesteads into cooperative farms, which revitalised the traditional communal ways of life. These Ujamaa villages were supplied with electricity and clean water, schools and clinics to encourage peasants to produce more food for the nation. Rodney believed Ujamaa reduced Tanzania's reliance on trade with the

West by replacing cash crops with food farming. In one of his most controversial articles, he went as far as to claim that Ujamaa charted a new path to socialism that would be distinct from that of developed Western nations.

Rodney defended his view against some Marxists who argued that a socialist revolution could only happen in Western capitalist countries, which had a large modern industry and therefore a large working class. They believed underdeveloped nations like Tanzania must first experience years of capitalist development before a workers' struggle for socialism would become conceivable. But they overlooked that the Russian Revolution, the only sustained victory of the proletariat over the bourgeoisie, unfolded in an underdeveloped country where the working class accounted for only 3 percent of the population. Therefore, Rodney was right to argue against these Marxists that Tanzanians could fight for socialism in the present rather than suffer under more decades of capitalism. But he overplayed his hand when he claimed that Tanzanian socialism could occur without a workers' revolution.

Rodney assigned no significant role to the Tanzanian working class because he thought the peasant Ujamaa villages alone could form the basis of a socialist society that avoided capitalism, if TANU modernised them with help from other socialist nations. He hoped this route would safeguard peasants against the inequalities that colonialism produced through individual commercial farming—the rise of landlords at the expense of landless peasants. By socialism, he meant preserving the Ujamaa villages from capitalist influence. However, he failed to see that leaving the working class out of the equation would have adverse consequences for the realisation of socialism in Tanzania.

Until 1973, Rodney supported the Tanzanian state as the driver of socialism and the peasantry as its base. He discarded the central idea of Marxism that the emancipation of the working class must be the act of the workers. In Tanzania, the working class was too small and unorganised to lead the nation out of poverty. He naively expected Nyerere and TANU to deliver socialism to the peasants and workers and to share state power with them. Failing to see the masses as capable of liberating themselves, he thus favoured a form of socialism from above. But his enthusiasm for Tanzanian socialism vanished the more he looked at the bureaucratic class that controlled TANU and the state. In 1978, four years after he left Tanzania, Rodney declared: "TANU has not been transformed. It remains a nationalist party under the control of the petit-bourgeoisie... incapable of providing the basis for sustained socialist transformation" (Quoted in Leo Zeilig, 'Walter Rodney's Journey to Hamburg', *Review of African Political Economy* blog, 2019).

Why did Rodney change his mind in less than five years? His Marxist USARF comrades played a key role in convincing him that TANU's Ujamaa villages and nationalised factories failed to empower the peasants and workers. They thought these policies allowed the Tanzanian one-party state to exploit and oppress the masses as under colonialism. From late 1973, Rodney also realised this when he looked at TANU's catastrophic plan to increase Ujamaa villages to stop the food shortage that had hit the countryside. TANU ordered peasants to move to areas that were unsuitable for farming. It then deployed the police when the peasants refused to relocate. That the bureaucrats never sought to persuade the peasant disheartened Rodney. He was even more appalled to learn from his discussions with peasants that they controlled no aspects of production in Ujamaa villages. All that mattered for TANU was how much grain it could quickly extract from the peasants' labour. Reflecting on these experiences he warned: "It is always dangerous for bureaucratisation to parade in the name of socialism. It happened under Stalin" (Walter Rodney, 'Class Contradictions in Tanzania', in *The State in Tanzania*, Dar es Salaam University Press, 1980). He feared that TANU, which had led the masses out of colonialism, had now begun to act like any Stalinist one-party bureaucratic state.

Rodney was also struck by TANU's contempt for workers as it refused to extend management of its nationalised factories to them. Although Tanzanian bureaucrats had replaced colonial managers, workers remained exploited on low wages. He disliked that Nyerere described workers as a privileged class, accusing them of wanting to steal from the peasants when they asked for higher wages. Nyerere had forced workers to sacrifice their interests in favour of national unity. Back in 1964 he co-opted all trade unions into the one-party state after labour leaders supported an army mutiny against him. The mistreatment of the masses led Rodney to grow suspicious of the petty bourgeois class who ran TANU—the students, intellectuals and civil servants that colonialism had educated. In 1975, he explained that the petty bourgeoisie never owned anything until it seized the colonial state after independence. The state became its lever of power as it took bureaucratic ownership of the economy from the British and Asian traders. Rodney now saw the Ujamaa villages and national factories not as socialism, but as a means for TANU's petty bourgeoisie to expand state control over production and to recruit more of its kind into lucrative bureaucratic jobs. TANU, he concluded, could not be reformed from within.

How could the masses free themselves from their exploitation at the hands of the state? Rodney found his solution when he looked back and rejoiced at the workers' strike movement of the early 1970s. In 1975, four months after he left Tanzania, Rodney spoke to students in Chicago about the conflicts between the masses and the weak Tanzania state, enthusiastically declaring those workers' struggles threatened TANU with revolution. He argued that the Tanzanian working class was small but its strategic position in the economy gave it great power. Nyerere and TANU could not ignore the agitation of workers in the factories, the docks and in the hospitals. The state, as Rodney explained, issued a charter of workers' rights in 1971 called Mwongozo to respond to workers' demands for better conditions. The charter stipulated that employers couldn't be arrogant, contemptuous and oppressive, as they had been under colonialism. But TANU's efforts to appease workers backfired. The workers went beyond TANU's expectations by using the charter to contest low wages, favouritism and sexual harassment. They printed and kept a booklet version of the charter and opened it on the appropriate page when arguing with management. When the petty bourgeoisie refused to apply the charter in the workplace, the workers led strikes and occupations to implement the Mwongozo charter.

In a speech he gave in Hamburg in 1978, Rodney drew even more radical conclusions from his reflections on these workers' struggles. He showed that the strikes of the early 1970s were not organised by the official trade unions—they were wildcat strikes spontaneously organised by the rank-and-file. He saw in them a new source of power that challenged TANU's state-led socialism. Rodney reflected on instances where workers' struggles went beyond demands for wages to ask: "Who should control production? Who is the boss in a so-called socialist society?" In one rubber factory, he explained, the workers locked out management and ran the factory causing panic and fear among the bureaucracy. The workers realised their power when they said: "We as workers are capable of running this enterprise more efficiently than the economic bureaucracy." The petty bourgeoisie crushed these revolts, fearing that they could spread across factories and destroy its existence as a class. Rodney had realised that workers had developed a revolutionary consciousness through their own experience of struggle—they had the power to propose a new democratic and collective way of organising society. Rodney thus returned to the core contention of Marxism, that the working class is the only class that can liberate itself and the whole of society. If Nyerere and TANU could not deliver socialism, it had to be won from below.

★ 8: RODNEY'S VIEWS ON PAN-AFRICANISM (1974)

Leaders from Africa and the diaspora gathered in Nyerere's Tanzania to attend the Sixth Pan African Congress in June 1974. It was the first time an African nation had hosted the Congress. Black intellectuals of the diaspora had organised previous ones in Europe. Rodney, however, was disappointed with Nyerere for refusing to allow grassroots organisations from participating in the debates. He feared the Congress would reflect the conservatism of African leaders unable to offer radical solutions to Africa's problems. So he wrote a provocative article for the event to address the key issue of African unity and denounce the impotence of petty bourgeois leaders.

In his article, Rodney conceived of Pan-Africanism as a weapon in the struggle against imperialism. It was less an ideology than a historical movement to unite Africans beyond the artificial borders that colonialism had created. He was appalled that most independent nations accepted these colonial borders. If Africa remained fragmented, it would stay vulnerable to incursion from Western companies seeking to rob its wealth. He argued the Pan-Africanism of "the petty bourgeois states became a sterile formulation... incapable of challenging capitalism and imperialism" (Walter Rodney, 'Aspects of the International Class Struggle in African, the Caribbean and America' in *Pan-Africanism: Struggle against Neo-colonialism and Imperialism*, Afro-Carib Publications, Toronto, 1975). He therefore saw the Organisation of African Unity (OAU), the predecessor of the African Union, as a club for African heads of state destined to betray the masses. The OAU, created in 1963, at best regulated conflicts between African dictators while it sanctified existing borders to ensure that the elite kept ruling over the masses in their own states.

Rodney's article offered insight into the treacherous and cowardly nature of the class that ruled Africa after independence. The petty bourgeoisie, he said, once played a progressive role by leading the anti-colonial struggle and voicing its support for Pan-Africanism. But it reneged on African unity when it negotiated independence, lacking the vision and the economic power to enforce that unity. Rodney here echoed Frantz Fanon who argued that the petty bourgeoisie owns nothing and will provide nothing. Apart from Nyerere and Ghana's Kwame Nkrumah, most leaders sought to get rich by becoming agents of the Western bourgeoisie, never seeking to defy imperialism. The petty bourgeoisie's control over the state—the police, the army and the bureaucracy—meant it had a vested interest in maintaining colonial borders. That way Africa's new ruling classes ensured that multinationals dealt with them, and that workers and peasants stayed oppressed and exploited.

Seeing the petty bourgeoisie as the biggest obstacle towards African unity, Rodney argued that Pan-Africanism had to become a movement driven from below. He called on Africans to struggle against the Western capitalist class and its African allies, to break from imperialism and build a socialist society that would free the masses from exploitation. Which class was to lead that struggle? In 1974, Rodney's article did not give a definitive answer. He believed that Pan-Africanism had to be an internationalist, anti-imperialist and socialist weapon in the hands of progressive groups and organisations. He saw the seeds of a new leadership in the guerrilla struggles and emerging workers' movement in Southern Africa when he wrote: "Our brothers in the south are striking blows, which include attacks on enemy bases in Angola, the destruction of rail links in Mozambique, the disruption of production through strikes in Namibia and South Africa." In time, he would come to believe that the working class in Africa and the Global South was the only class able to lead an African liberation struggle to socialism.

Rodney fell ill before the Pan-African Congress and was unable to attend and deliver his powerful article. Moreover, he thought it was time for him to return to Guyana. Rodney thought he would never be able to fully relate to Tanzanians and grasp their idiom. He told one of his students: "I have to go back to people I know and who know me." Rodney had made important contributions to the African liberation struggle, which inspired countless radical African students and intellectuals. But he was only an academic moving in academic circles. He was discontented with being a radical intellectual—he wanted to be a revolutionary. He longed to build a close relationship with working people and play an integral part in their struggles against exploitation. He felt that could only be done back home.

★9: A DIFFICULT RETURN TO GUYANA (1974-1976)

In Guyana, a multiracial gathering was a rare sight. Yet, in August 1974, between two and three thousand African and Indian Guyanese rallied in front of the University of Georgetown to support Walter Rodney. They had heard that Prime Minister Forbes Burnham's regime had pressured the university to overturn his appointment as head of the history department. Angered by that decision, the university staff union and students boycotted classes for two weeks, while the Guyanese Bar Association went on strike. Many intellectuals launched a global campaign to reinstate Rodney, who had gained an international reputation for his scholarship on African history. Rodney had not even left Tanzania, yet he was already the focus of protests and a major political issue for the Guyanese government. Burnham and his cronies feared him because of his past activism in Jamaica and his popularity among the Guyanese masses. Rodney was an advocate of racial solidarity and a Marxist critic of the government, which divided the Guyanese along racial lines and kept them in poverty. He knew he would return to a country that was different from the one of his childhood.

Rodney had left Guyana at 18 years of age and did not

live through its decline into racial violence. The racial solidarity of the anti-colonial movement crumbled after the British overthrew the People's Progressive Party's (PPP) government in a coup in 1953. The coup produced a split between the PPP's two leaders, the African lawyer Forbes Burnham and the Indian dentist Cheddi Jagan. Burnham now accused Jagan of being "a communist stooge" and left to create the People's National Congress (PNC) in 1957. The ideological split turned into a racial one as both parties mobilised for elections on the basis of racial loyalty. Indians remained in the PPP while Africans joined the PNC. The PPP won the 1957 and 1961 legislative and local elections because it relied on the votes from the Indo-Guyanese majority. The Cold War, however, interfered again in Guyanese politics to ensure the PPP's defeat in 1964. The CIA financed a coalition between Burnham's PNC and the smaller United Force, which represented the local Portuguese and Chinese capitalists. The Americans wanted to prevent Jagan from turning Guyana into a second Cuba, once it became independent from Britain. Thus, Burnham's coalition led Guyana to independence in 1966 because of his close relations with the United States.

The electoral campaigns revived old tensions between Africans and Indians, which culminated in violent clashes between 1961 and 1964. The deadliest confrontations unfolded in the spring of 1964 when the colonial government sent African scabs to break the strike of Indian sugar workers. Ten years later, the bitterness and animosity between African and Indian communities had not disappeared. The semblance of racial harmony that the PNC's propaganda tried to convey was obscured by the glaring fact that Burnham and the Afro-Guyanese bureaucracy dominated the state and continued to discriminate against Indians. This was the country that Rodney returned to in September 1974.

Patricia and the children, who had relocated before Rodney, welcomed Rodney upon his arrival in Georgetown. The family struggled to adjust to life in Guyana. Patricia missed her African friends and the hospitality she encountered in Tanzania. She disliked that people did not greet each other in Guyana and that her children were bullied in school because of their African names and accents. Patricia was also refused employment in healthcare when hiring managers found out that she was married to Rodney. Yet, she secured a job and a house in spite of the government's hostility towards her husband. Rodney, however, was jobless as the protests of August 1974 had failed to achieve his reinstatement at the university. He earned a little from lectures he gave overseas and teaching at Cornell University from January to May 1975. But he decided to stay in Guyana and fight Burnham's despotism.

Interviewed in 1976, Rodney accused the government of using control over jobs to intimidate people. "This control is important," he said, "we are a small undeveloped economy with a large unemployed sector—to retain one's job is a matter of life or death" (Dr David Hinds, *In the Sky's Wild Noise: A Documentary on Dr Walter Rodney*, 2014, available on Youtube). He also claimed Guyanese workers could not seek work elsewhere because the state had become the largest employer. Burnham's regime had nationalised 80 percent of the economy, which included the bauxite mines and sugar plantations. This takeover of foreign companies represented Burnham's opportunistic shift in ideology to what Rodney called pseudo-socialism. Burnham had reneged on his earlier anti-communism and alliance with the United States when Guyana's production and exports had fallen. Burnham now looked to Cuba and China for economic assistance and declared Guyana a 'Socialist Cooperative Republic'. Burnham's ideological zigzag enabled him to promote himself as a progressive leader abroad, though his citizens saw him as a dictator.

Burnham and the PNC kept stoking the tensions between Africans and Indians to divert attention from its failure to provide jobs, transport and decent health care. They rigged elections and granted senior bureaucratic positions to Africans while purging their opponents. The state shot and arrested PPP activists and blamed Indian sugar workers for stealing the nation's revenue when they went on strike. The key issue of racism in Guyana preoccupied Rodney who spent his days writing articles and speeches on that question. He travelled across the country, conducted interviews among his people and researched archives for his famous book, *A History of the Guyanese Working People 1880-1905*. Rodney's formidable body of work provided a Marxist explanation for the divide between Africans and Indians.

10: RACE, CLASS AND GUYANESE POLITICS

Rodney's writings and speeches on race and class in Guyanese history explained how capitalist exploitation created the conditions for modern racism. Speaking on this topic at Columbia University in 1978, Rodney presented racism as a product of capitalism when it developed as a global system in the 1600s. Europe's ruling class invented racism to justify African slavery in the New World to produce goods for the world market. Racism, he said, always stems from the interests of the exploitative classes. This meant that the racism between Guyanese African and Indians workers was not a matter of natural prejudice or cultural difference. In fact, this divide originated in the colonial plantation society, which brought Africans as slaves and then Indians as indentured workers. As a Marxist, Rodney regarded racism in Guyana as the consequence of the white planter class's divide and rule strategy to control labour after the abolition of slavery in 1838. He gained that insight from his analysis of Guyanese history, whereby he recognised the material conditions for the existence of racism under capitalism.

First, Rodney identified that racial tensions among workers arose out of competition over jobs on plantations in the decade after emancipation. In his article *Plantation Society in Guyana* and his *History of the Guyanese Working People*, Rodney explained that most ex-slaves became plantation workers and fought the planters over decent wages and working conditions. They even organised two general strikes right after emancipation. Although the strike of 1841 was victorious, that of 1847 failed because the planters imported indentured Indians as scabs. The white planter class had introduced cheap and precarious labour from India in an attempt to break the rising African militancy. Rodney also argued that Indian indentureship created excess labour in British Guyana, which enabled the planters to use unemployment to control the workforce. If Africans refused the terms of employment, they feared Indians might replace them. At the same time, as Rodney notes, indentured immigration split the working class. African workers tended to perform skilled labour, such as cane cutting, while the Indians did the menial tasks.

Secondly, Rodney saw that racist ideas, which came from the white planter class, appealed to African and Indian workers. Racism offered them a false sense of comfort in the face of the exploitation and misery they endured in the colony. The economic competition on the plantation meant that African workers despised Indians as job stealers and tools of the planters. Conversely, Indians saw Africans as lazy workers who would have starved without indenture. As Rodney claimed, they "began to relate to each other via the white (planter) stereotype" (Walter Rodney, *A History of the Guyanese Working People, 1881-1905*, Johns Hopkins University Press, Baltimore, 1981).

Thirdly, Rodney identified that all ruling classes in

Guyana deliberately took advantage of the racial tension between Africans and Indians. He argued that the policy of the colonial state was aimed at ensuring that both races policed each other—by using one racial group to quell the resistance of the other. Rodney quoted one planter who understood that the safety of his class relied upon maintaining the animosity between Africans and Indians: "If the Negroes were troublesome every coolie (Indian) on the estate would stand by one. If the coolies attacked me, I could with confidence trust my Negro friends to keep me from injury" (*History of the Guyanese Working People*, p189). This 'divide and rule', which separated and weakened workers in the face of exploitation, meant that the wages in Guyana stagnated from the 1840s until the end of indenture in 1920.

In his speech at Columbia University, Rodney claimed the African and Indian elite of the 1970s drew on the old racist manipulation to defend their interests as rulers. He explained that the African middle class emerged, through the colonial schooling offered in towns, as teachers, junior civil servants and sometimes lawyers. The Indian elite, however, emerged from the plantations as landlords and merchants. The African elite, which saw itself as the heir to the colonial state, opposed the Indian elite who also wanted state power to support its businesses. From the 1930s to the 1970s, both elites used racism to mobilise their communities against each other as they battled for control of the state. Burnham's regime, for instance, revived the old stereotypes of Indians being greedy to vilify the 135-day strike of Indian sugar workers of 1977-78, while he recruited thousands of African scabs to break the strike.

The racial politics of African and Indian elites also served as a mechanism to reinforce solidarity within their respective communities. Rodney argued that the Indian landlord farmers, who grew wealthy from callously exploiting their fellow Indians, were ironically often spiritual leaders and the most vocal defenders of Indian interests against Africans. Likewise, Burnham bragged about belonging to the African community while oppressing his own people. By mobilising on the basis of race, both elites could hide the class differences between them and their workers.

The Guyanese people, however, did not always accept the racist manipulation of their rulers. Rodney observed that while the class struggle was fragmented in the 1800s, African and Indian workers often united against their bosses in the following century. He devoted the final chapter of his *History of the Guyanese Working People* to the 1905 rebellion. Indian sugar workers had mounted a strike that spread to the African cane cutters and stevedores, setting the stage for an unprecedented multiracial alliance. But the colonial state rushed to crush the revolt before the alliance took shape. 1905 proved to Rodney that racial unity was possible on the basis of class struggle. By fighting for higher wages, African and Indian workers started to realise their common interests and overcame their racial prejudices. At Columbia University, Rodney mentioned that workers united again in the strikes of 1924, 1938 and the 1950s during the anti-colonial movement. He pointed out that colonial governors saw this workers' unity as the biggest threat to the colony. And he predicted that it would be the Achilles heel of Burnham's dictatorship. Rodney's Marxist writings on race and class promoted the idea that racism could only be abolished through a revolution that united African and Indian workers against their exploiters.

While Rodney admired the spontaneity of Guyana's multiracial strikes, he also saw their shortcomings. The ruling class reversed the solidarity the strikes had engendered when it restored order. Rodney concluded that workers' spontaneous struggles needed to be channelled by an organisation. His concern was how African and Indian workers could forge an irreversible bond through organisation. In this respect, he saw the anti-colonial alliance of the 1950s as a fragile one, resting on the electoral ambitions of Jagan and Burnham. Rodney aspired to politicise the masses in ways that had not been done before. So, he joined the Working People's Alliance in 1976 to fight racism and the Guyanese dictatorship.

★ 11: THE BIRTH OF THE WORKING PEOPLE'S ALLIANCE

The racial conflict in Guyana produced a political system that only allowed space for Burnham's PNC and its opposition, Jagan's PPP. Both parties preached a version of socialism from above that favoured the petty bourgeoisie's control over the state, never the masses. Burnham blatantly discriminated against the Indo-Guyanese, while Jagan talked about racial unity but, when it came to elections, only campaigned among Indians. In 1974, amidst this political deadlock, the Working People's Alliance (WPA) emerged as an anti-racist and anti-imperialist formation that advocated for socialism from below. It was not an electoral party, but a small pressure group that united Pan-Africanist and Indian socialist organisations aspiring to build mass action against Burnham's dictatorship. Rodney, however, joined the WPA as one of its few independent members. He befriended Eusi Kwayana, the group's co-founder and a well-known Pan-African activist, who had left both the PPP and PNC out of disgust for their racial politics and their corruption. Many of the WPA co-founders had also grown disillusioned with the major parties and sought a new politics to overcome the racial divide among the working masses. Rodney's uncompromising use of

Marxist theory and practice to foster working class unity helped them to find it.

One of the WPA's first major anti-racist interventions occurred when it defended an Indian PPP activist Arnold Rampersaud, who the PNC had framed for the murder of an African policeman. At the solidarity rally, Rodney gave a moving speech calling on the Afro-Guyanese to resist Burnham's attempt to manipulate them against the Indians. When a policeman ordered Rodney to stop speaking, the multiracial audience surged forward, removed the officer, and allowed Rodney to finish his speech. Thus began his transformation into a full-time organiser of the working people. The Guyanese respected Rodney as a Marxist scholar and activist, still unaware that he was soon to become their foremost leader.

Rodney and the WPA established bases. They led reading groups and spoke at public meetings in Georgetown and in the bauxite mining regions. Rodney enjoyed lecturing miners on Marxist political economy and the Russian Revolution of 1917 as well as discussing Guyanese politics and labour conditions in the bauxite regions. The WPA's influence among the Indian sugar workers was less notable because it did not seek to infringe upon the territory of their allies, the PPP. The WPA considered the PPP allies because it was the main opposition to Burnham's regime and the main political force within the Guyanese labour movement. It derived the largest share of its support from the Indian sugar workers and their trade unions. Although the WPA knew very well that Jagan's PPP represented a false alternative to Burnham's regime, it still sought to work with them. Rodney and his comrades understood that operating alongside the PPP would allow the WPA to spread its ideas of racial unity and its advocacy for rebellion against Burnham among PPP supporters to draw them closer to its radical politics.

WPA encountered several difficulties when trying to find common ground with the PPP. By 1975, the PPP had changed its attitude towards the PNC following Burnham's ideological shift from anti-communism to pro-communism. It no longer argued for 'non-cooperation and civil disobedience' against the PNC but now declared 'critical support' for it. The PPP's new political line was the consequence of the advice it received from the Soviet Union, which did not want to see two socialist parties in conflict with each other. As a result, the PPP decided to support Burnham's nationalisation programme and abandon all boycotts of the rigged parliament. In 1977, the PPP even proposed a National Patriotic Front Government where it would share parliamentary power with the PNC. Burnham, however, rejected the proposal after a series of futile negotiations.

The eruption of the 135-day strike of 1977 and 1978, the longest in Guyanese history, afforded the WPA an opportunity to engage with Indian sugar workers, which generally supported the PPP. The WPA successfully convinced African miners to donate in support of the 21,000 striking Indian plantation workers. Its collection for the strike relief challenged the idea that all Africans were scabs, especially after Burnham had sent unemployed Afro-Guyanese to replace or terrorise the strikers. The PPP-backed Guyanese Agricultural Workers' Union, which had called the strike, invited WPA members to speak at their public meeting. Rodney's speech again impressed the workers. The crowd grew bigger and bigger and overflowed onto the streets as he spoke about racial unity. When the WPA speakers left to attend another rally nearby they were surprised to see that the crowd had followed them.

Although the WPA relied on only a few dozen activists it escaped the most critical pitfalls of sectarianism that Rodney had observed among many small groups on the British revolutionary left in the 1960s. Whereas these sects used complex jargon and concepts that alienated British workers, the WPA with its slogan 'bread and justice' spoke to the Guyanese workers in a language they could understand. The WPA often refrained from declaring its socialist ideology in public to set itself apart from the PNC's abuse of the term socialism. More importantly, sectarianism meant that British sects failed to build links with mass movements, preferring to latch on to their empty socialist dogma—even if that meant isolation from the working class. The WPA, on the contrary, looked to foster mass support and action against Burnham's government by building and participating in broad coalitions and campaigns. In 1978, they campaigned with the PPP, trade unions and civic organisations to boycott the PNC's referendum to reform the constitution and extend Burnham's presidential powers. The regime nevertheless declared victory in the referendum, despite the low voter turnout.

Alliance building, however, presented another pitfall for the WPA—that of entering the wrong kind of alliance. In 1977, the WPA fell into that trap when it welcomed the PPP's futile proposal for a National Patriotic Front Government, though it had its reservations. Shortly after the WPA became a political party in 1979, it proposed a multi-party Government of National Unity and Reconstruction. There was a noteworthy difference between the proposals: the PPP wanted to share power with Burnham's PNC, while the WPA wanted to overthrow the PNC regime and replace it with a caretaker government of progressive forces. However, both proposals rested upon the belief that "all classes in Guyana had an objective interest in national unity" as Rodney declared in one of speeches. This view was mistaken. The objective interest of workers—their self-emancipation from exploitation—never could be reconciled with that of the petty bourgeoisie, which hoped to exploit Guyanese labour.

While the WPA's anti-referendum campaign of 1978 was an alliance between working class and grassroots organisations over specific aims, its proposal for national unity governments sought to include organisations of the petty bourgeoisie (businessmen, big farmers, civil servants, barristers) to form a bourgeois government.

It envisaged a long-term cooperation between classes around a liberal programme that consisted of restoring the national economy, civil liberties and the rule of law. Such a programme contradicted the WPA's socialist aspirations as it implied the subordination of its socialism from below to bourgeois parliamentary politics. If any of the national unity government plans of the 1970s had materialised, they likely would have had tragic outcomes for the WPA in the advent of a major popular uprising. Rodney and his comrades would have found themselves caught between workers' struggles and the petty bourgeoisie's desire to restore order. Would they have defended national unity against the workers?

The WPA made mistakes but it was not afraid to experiment. Through trial and error, it gradually rooted itself among the working people and played an increasing role in their struggles. The organisation produced a single newssheet called *Dayclean*, which its members regularly distributed at protests, rallies and door-to-door. This newssheet did not stop at exposing the dreadful conditions of the working people. It provided a critical overview of Burnham's state capitalism, of racism in Guyana and outlined the significance of popular struggles against it. As Burnham's PNC banned all free press, the WPA found it difficult to turn *Dayclean* into a substantial newspaper. The police raided its offices, seized all ink and printers and arrested those who sold the paper. The WPA, however, heroically strove to print *Dayclean* when possible, alongside pamphlets and manifestos that reflected its socialist ideology—to lead the revolution in each country, promote women's rights and education, fight against racism and build a classless society. The rise of the civil rebellion of 1979 would encourage the WPA to transform itself into a mass revolutionary party that would pose as a real alternative to Burnham and Jagan.

★12: THE CIVIL REBELLION, THE WPA AND THE WORKING PEOPLE.

At around 2am on 11 July 1979 someone set the Ministry of National Development in Georgetown on fire. Burnham knew who to blame for the arson, though he had no proof. In the afternoon, the police arrested Walter Rodney and six other WPA members. The dictator hoped to silence his opponents, but little did he know that the arrest would turn the WPA into a mass party with Rodney as the people's leader. When news of the arson spread across the country, working people in Georgetown, on the cane fields and in the mining communities gathered to discuss and condemn Rodney's arrest. In the capital, hundreds joined the WPA's pickets in front of prisons to identify the whereabouts of the prisoners and to campaign for their freedom.

On 14 July, thousands rallied in front of the courthouse demanding bail for the arrested. So great was the outcry that the judge agreed to release the WPA leaders against the PNC's wishes. Upon hearing the news, the multiracial protesters marched in triumph through Georgetown. All the political parties and organisations that opposed Burnham's dictatorship figured among those who supported the WPA. But the euphoric mood quickly vanished. Burnham deployed the armed militia of a religious group, the House of Israel, to break up the demonstration. The attackers stabbed a British Jesuit journalist Bernard Darke to death and wounded two WPA members. State repression did not tame the masses but fuelled them with rage. They initiated the civil rebellion against the PNC.

From July to November 1979, mass protests and strikes shook the PNC dictatorship. The people expressed their anger at the cuts in wages, healthcare and transport that the PNC had imposed in order to reimburse the loans from the International Monetary Fund (IMF) in 1978. They held the government responsible for the high unemployment rates, which stood at 30 percent. Faced with deteriorating living standards and lacking democratic rights, they could no longer tolerate the corruption that plagued the ruling party. Burnham grew nervous upon learning that African miners mounted a strike that paralysed the bauxite industry. It was the first time he faced a major rebellion among his African support base. The miners' strike against the public sector wage freeze also spread to parts of the civil service. At first, Burnham refused to declare the strike illegal, as he usually did, not wanting to frustrate the many PNC trade unionists who were involved. But Burnham's greatest fear became reality when 20,000 Indian sugar workers struck in solidarity with the miners a month later. Faced with the prospect of a multiracial general strike, Burnham and his cronies felt that power was slipping out of their hands.

In the pamphlet he wrote during the rebellion,

People's Power, No Dictator, Rodney told the masses about the central importance of strikes for advancing the political struggle against the dictatorship:

> United strike action teaches us how the dictator can be exposed and how he can be deposed... The dictator requires the population to produce so as to sustain himself and the clique of parasites who dominate Guyana. That is why the mass withdrawal of labour is the ultimate weapon representing the power of the people (Walter Rodney, 'People's Power, No Dictator' in *Latin American Perspectives*, Vol. 8, No.1, 1979, pp.64-77).

Rodney and the WPA tried to ensure that people supported the strikes through their individual and collective acts of resistance to Burnham. On 20 July the WPA organised its largest ever rally which attracted 8,000 people to the Bourda Mall, an open space where public meetings and markets were held in Georgetown. Rodney delivered a fiery speech in which he declared: "The PNC must go by any means necessary." The Guyanese people were amazed to hear someone articulate their feelings with such honesty and courage. A week later the WPA established itself as a political party geared towards the conquest of state power. Rodney and his comrades understood that the rebellion called on them to connect and direct all the struggles that had erupted in the towns, mines and the countryside. They aimed to transform these localised struggles over wages and democratic rights into general ones against the dictatorship. And they knew this task meant doing more extensive organising and agitation among the working people than before.

Before becoming a political party, the WPA had strict conditions of membership and stressed discipline and ideological unity among its dozens of volunteer cadre. Having a tight-knit organisation of a few trustworthy members was necessary to withstand harassment from Burnham's authoritarian regime. There was no mass movement behind which the WPA members could hide. It therefore had to rely on its trained cadres to constantly carry out operations while facing the threat of police infiltrators and raids. The WPA's ability to survive these difficult circumstances was the result of the meticulous planning of its leaders and the political education of its members.

Now, in the wake of the civil rebellion of 1979, the WPA leaders abandoned their strict recruitment policy. They opened their party's membership to the hundreds of Africans and Indians of all ages and social backgrounds that asked to join them as long as they agreed with its principles and rules. The WPA leadership had shown an astonishing degree of flexibility and audacity by overcoming the organisation's old habits, routines and fears of police spies. It derived its newfound determination to grow its ranks and lead the struggle from the large attendance, the electric applause and the ovations that the WPA received at its public meetings. The WPA still maintained its emphasis on the political training of its membership and the formation of a revolutionary cadre. It created education classes and branches called "nuclei" for its party members and organisers, where they read radical literature, such as Lenin's *What is to Be Done* and Amilcar Cabral's *Party Principles and Political Practices*.

What did the WPA stand for? "The alliance is revolutionary and not reformist," it asserted in its programme. The WPA meant that socialism could only be achieved through the self-emancipatory struggles of the oppressed masses against their rulers. Rodney expressed this idea when he said: "The revolution is made by ordinary people, not by angels, it's made by people from all walks of life, and more particularly by the working class who are in the majority" (Walter Rodney, *Sign of the Times*, Working People's Alliance, Guyana, 1981). It therefore rejected the idea that a small group of enlightened and benevolent leaders could gradually deliver socialism to the passive and grateful masses. This understanding made the WPA different from the PNC who identified 'socialism' with state ownership of the economy by a handful of bureaucrats. It also made the WPA different from the PPP, which saw elections— winning a majority in the Assembly and passing laws—as the means to deliver socialist change. The WPA also opposed the cult of personality that had evolved around Forbes Burnham and Cheddi Jagan. "We profoundly distrust the Messiah approach of political parties," said Rodney. "We are trying to mobilise the energies of the vast majority of the population." Unlike the PNC or PPP, the WPA established a collective leadership of 15 members, with a rotating chairmanship to ensure that nobody monopolised power.

There was a striking resemblance between the WPA's claim to see "the revolution in each country as permanent" and Leon Trotsky's theory of permanent revolution. Seventy years before, the Russian revolutionary had argued that, even in underdeveloped countries, the fight for democratic rights could grow over into a struggle to expropriate the capitalists and create a socialist society, provided the working class led the revolution with the support of the oppressed. By permanent revolution Trotsky further meant spreading the revolution beyond national borders. However, there was also reason to believe that Trotsky's theory did not influence WPA intellectuals. While Trotsky conceived revolution as a fluid process, the WPA expected it to present two distinct stages in Guyana, which supposed the realisation of a democratic state as a pre-condition for socialist change.

The WPA programme nevertheless did converge with Trotsky's ideas in several ways. First, it recognised the leading role of the working class in the revolutionary process. Second, it stressed the need for an alliance between workers and peasants. The WPA programme of 1978 voiced democratic demands such as land for the peasants, the right to work, and freedom of the press. These accompanied its calls for workers' control over the factories and the creation of workers' assemblies as new ruling organs. Third, the WPA was committed to internationalism. It built ties with the Grenadian socialists who overthrew their dictator in March 1979 and sent WPA members to help with the Grenadian Revolution. That year, the WPA observed with excitement the Sandinista revolution in Nicaragua, the Iranian Revolution and the Surinamese coup d'état. The rise of the civil rebellion offered its members hope that Guyana was next in line.

WPA leader Eusi Kwayana said that the rebellion "saw almost the whole society creeping out of the shadows into the light of hope, standing in defiance of the power that was ... imposing economic and financial oppression and hardship" (*Guyana Under Siege: Walter Rodney*, 1988 available at guyanaundersiege.com/leaders/rodney3.htm).

The mass rallies that the WPA organised at the height of the rebellion turned into spontaneous marches. In the countryside and the towns, people took to the streets drumming and chanting their favourite slogan: "People Power, No Dictator". Rodney's activism was relentless during the rebellion. He travelled throughout the country to organise and speak at rallies. People promoted his meetings by word of mouth, never with leaflets. He appeared, spoke and captivated the masses, then left before the police or Burnham's thugs could catch him. His speeches broke the wall of silence and fear around the dictatorship as he mocked Burnham, baptising him "King Kong". Rodney thus emerged out of Guyana's highest moment of struggle as the key revolutionary leader of the people.

★ 13: RODNEY'S DEATH AND AFTERMATH

In November 1979, Rodney spoke at a meeting on the corner of Lamaha Street in Georgetown. But the PNC's armed thugs stormed the gathering and chased Rodney through a district of the capital. Rodney escaped after hiding in a sewage trench and then reached his friend's home "smelling like an unwashed ram goat". It was not the first time Rodney had to run for his life but the ferocity of his assailants signalled that Burnham wanted to eliminate his opposition at any cost. Rodney was able to escape this time. Some of his comrades were not so fortunate. The Guyana Police Force shot and killed leading WPA member Ohene Koama on 18 November. Koama was the first WPA activist to die at the hands of the state, and his death signalled a decline in the civil rebellion.

Rodney observed signs of the movement's retreat as the state's repression made it difficult for the WPA to organise in the streets. The police sabotaged the WPA's cars and speaking equipment and detained Rodney on three occasions between September and October. Rodney and the other WPA leaders knew the mass meetings and protests of the summer had shielded them from onslaughts from the state. But the vanishing struggle left them exposed. When the Burnham regime threatened to bomb their home, Rodney and his wife Patricia moved their family to different safe homes on a nightly basis.

Other WPA members also moved from safe house to safe house to avoid police raids and harassment as they tried to come to terms with the ebb of the civil rebellion.

Eusi Kwayana argued that the civil rebellion retreated with the collapse of workers' strikes, which he saw as the backbone of the movement. There was frustration among the WPA leaders as the united action of the miners and sugar workers failed to grow into a general strike. The WPA was not rooted among the sugar workers and was unable to raise their combativeness, as they still suffered from the defeat of their 135-day strike in 1978. Its influence had not extended beyond the capital and some mining regions. In May 1980, Rodney criticised the defeatism of the leadership of the PPP, trade unions and anti-dictatorship groups who failed to grasp the destructive potential of the strikes and protests—they believed the regime would be left unshaken. The opportunistic PPP saw industrial action only as a platform for its electoral campaigns and as a lever for its negotiations with the PNC, while the trade union leaders lacked the confidence to withstand the threats from the state. After bullying the unions into submission, the state fired the most militant workers, replacing them with scab labour.

In the aftermath of the retreat of the civil rebellion, the WPA claimed that Guyana was not ripe for revolution because the armed forces had failed to join the protesters. Some of its leaders adjusted to the downturn by focusing on building new WPA branches and working towards a government of national unity. Yet, without the mass protests, the party was more exposed to Burnham's thugs who murdered a second WPA member, Edward Dublin, in February 1980. It is conceivable that the sheer repression from the PNC, during and after the civil rebellion, led Rodney and the WPA to consider armed resistance.

Three decades later, WPA leaders Rupert Roopnaraine and Tacuma Ogunseye disclosed that their party accumulated weapons during that period. Although Roopnaraine told filmmaker Clairmont Chung that the WPA was preparing itself and the masses for an insurrection, he never defined what he meant by insurrection. A few years later, Ogunseye explained that Rodney, Roopnaraine and himself formed a security committee that supplied 12 automatic guns to WPA underground cells for the party's self-defence. No other WPA activist has confirmed the claims of these leaders, and the PNC never rightfully charged any WPA member with handling weapons.

Regarding Rodney's alleged role in the WPA security committee, Ogunseye claimed that Rodney was building links with the army to prepare the ground for the military to join the masses in the next popular rebellion. Roopnaraine's account reveals another possible aspect of Rodney's activities at the time. He argued that Rodney ached to revive the mass movement out of fear it would forever disappear. In April 1980, he helped smuggle Rodney to neighbouring Suriname, so that Rodney could fly to Zimbabwe's independence celebrations and seek support and weapons to reignite the civil rebellion. When he received no such assistance, said Roopnaraine after visiting Rodney upon his return, "He (Rodney) was in a very low place, morale had dropped.... Walter was always very sensitive about the need for militancy" (Clairmont Chung, *Walter A. Rodney: A Promise of Revolution*, Monthly Review Press, New York, 2012, p111).

After his death, his mentor CLR James said that Rodney overestimated the inclination of the Guyanese people to take up arms against Burnham. James also presumed Rodney paid no attention to training WPA leaders and cadre in the art of insurrection—he instead wanted to lead by example and take his own risks. He also blamed the WPA for failing to keep Rodney away from the front lines. While there was space for armed resistance within Rodney's politics as he studied and admired the likes of Che Guevara and Frantz Fanon, it is unclear how he planned to respond to Burnham's repression. James was not in Guyana in the late 1970s, and therefore his knowledge of events was limited. Does his argument that Rodney undertook too much risk and that his comrades failed to protect him have any semblance of truth?

A part of the answer lies in the fact that many WPA leaders were unaware of the operations of the security committee though they knew about its existence. According to Roopnaraine, some resigned from the party's executive, disappointed by the lack of accountability from their peers, upon learning that Rodney had been smuggled to Zimbabwe. Furthermore, WPA leaders bore all the burden of secretly acquiring arms and equipment, of which a considerable amount came from the military. Roopnaraine said in conclusion: "We found ourselves at all hours of the night in strange places, doing dangerous things... the miracle is that more of us didn't get killed." But Burnham and the PNC murdered Rodney.

On 13 June 1980, Rodney and his brother Donald went to acquire walkie-talkies from an ex-army officer, Gregory Smith. They did not suspect that Smith was a PNC informant. When Rodney activated the device in his car, it exploded and killed him. The Guyanese working people mourned the loss of their leader while Burnham rejoiced. The next day the police and the army patrolled the streets fearing that Rodney's death would spark another uprising. They raided Rodney's mother's house searching for weapons, and anonymous leaflets appeared on the streets with a message: "He who lives by the bomb shall die by the bomb".

Rodney's funeral was the largest ever held in Guyana. Thirty-five to fifty thousand Guyanese of all races, ages and genders attended his funeral to wish their beloved leader farewell. Patricia led her husband's procession chanting 'Fight back, fight back'. Rodney once said that when revolutionaries fall, "they are lost, it's an irreparable loss that may... qualitatively affect the development of the struggle in another phase". His death represented that loss for socialist revolution in Guyana.

After Rodney was murdered, the WPA did its best to continue the struggle. It established bases across the country despite Burnham's repression. The party, however, gradually relinquished its revolutionary socialist programme to adopt an electoral strategy after Burnham's illness and death in the mid-1980s. The new strategy made it incapable of challenging the racial divide that still plagues Guyana today. The WPA never performed well in elections. The civil rebellion of 1979 had shown that African and Indian could shake off their racial prejudices and see one another as part of the same class when they engaged in united strikes and protests. In contrast with that collective struggle, elections counted on the passivity, uncertainty and individualism of a people who had been shaped by centuries of racial oppression.

Far from promoting the anti-racism of the small WPA, election campaigns galvanised existing racial divisions as leaders of the much larger PNC and PPP continued mobilising Africans and Indians against each other to win votes. Following the PPP's victories in Guyana's first free elections in 1992 and 1997, African PNC supporters attacked Indians, ransacked polling stations and clashed with the police. These tragic episodes of racial violence showed that real change could not be achieved through the ballot box.

All of Rodney's writing and activism in Guyana had underlined the centrality of class struggle for fighting racism. It's only by fighting against the ruling class in the streets and the workplaces that African and Indian workers could realise their common interest and overcome their prejudices. Every victory, big or small, could strengthen the confidence of the working class and encourage its unity against capital. Rodney saw a revolutionary party as essential for challenging racist ideas and for shaping the fight for socialism. If the workers failed to overcome their racial divide, they would be unable to defeat capitalism.

★ CONCLUSION: THE PROPHET OF SELF-EMANCIPATION

In his short biographical sketch of Rodney, WPA leader Eusi Kwayana identified Rodney as "the prophet of self-emancipation". Everywhere he went, Rodney fought alongside the working people, inspiring them to win their freedom. The more he travelled and engaged with the masses, the more he embraced Marxism as his theory and practice of working class revolution. Rodney's activism in Jamaica shaped his belief in the duty of revolutionary intellectuals to be involved in the struggle against imperialism and capitalism. Radical intellectuals do not belong in the university. They must go to the oppressed, learn about their struggles, and use their intellect for the struggle for liberation. Rodney followed this path by meeting with Rastafarians and listening to radical youths. His ability to understand and relate to the masses led him to deliver a powerful message of Black Power. He articulated the grievances of the masses while telling them to reclaim the Caribbean from imperialism and its local allies.

His progress from Black Power activism to socialism became apparent when he lived in Nyerere's Tanzania. Rodney used Marx's historical method to write his masterpiece *How Europe Underdeveloped Africa*. He produced a history of the exploitation of African workers and peasants by the Western bourgeoisie, to prove that Africa's development was impossible until it broke with capitalism. He left Tanzania convinced that enlightened leaders could not deliver socialism—it had to be won from below. Rodney had discovered in the strikes of Tanzania the unrivalled power and militancy of the working class. Only they had the power and the vision to build a new democratic society, a socialist one.

Rodney developed his appreciation of workers' power when he returned to Guyana and organised for the WPA. His writings, speeches and activism revealed the importance of Marxism for explaining and fighting racism. He saw racism as a product of capitalism, wherein capitalists divided the working class to ensure its exploitation. He proposed to end it with a revolution that united African and Indian workers against Burnham's dictatorship. Rodney then recognised the need for a mass revolutionary party to foster that racial unity. His WPA, which had grown its ranks from dozens to hundreds while bravely leading the struggle against Burnham in 1979, still did not have enough members, experience and influence to face the state repression and lead the civil rebellion to victory. If the mass party had established itself years before the rebellion, it perhaps would have been better prepared to influence the struggle. But the WPA never recovered from Rodney's death.

Although Rodney died at only 38 years of age, he left behind him a colossal body of work that will inspire the next generation of revolutionaries. That makes him the prophet of self-emancipation.

A GUIDE TO FURTHER READING

Most of Walter Rodney's main works are still in print including *A History of the Guyanese Working People, 1881-1905*, (John Hopkins University Press, Baltimore, Maryland, 1981), History of the Upper Guinea Coast, 1545-1800 (Monthly Review Press, New York, 1989) and *The Making of an African Intellectual* (Africa World Press, Trenton, New Jersey, 1990).

Verso books have also recently published a series of Walter Rodney's writings and collections of his lectures including *Groundings with my Brothers*, *How Europe Underdeveloped Africa*, *Decolonial Marxism* and *The Russian Revolution: A View From The Third World*.

Many of Walter Rodney's writings, including most of the shorter articles cited in the text, are available for free at the Marxists Internet Archive marxists.org. Many of the articles by other writers such as Amílcar Cabral, Che Guevara, CLR James and Tony Cliff can also be found at marxists.org

Rupert Lewis has produced two extensive studies: *Walter Rodney: 1968 Revisited*, (UWI Press, Kingston, 1988); and *Walter Rodney's Intellectual and Political Thought*, (UWI Press, Kingston, 1998).

Other books about Rodney's life include: *Clairmont Chung, Walter A. Rodney: A Promise of Revolution*, (Monthly Review Press, New York, 2012); Arnold Gibbons, *The Legacy of Walter Rodney in Guyana and the Caribbean* (University Press of America, Lanham, Maryland, 2012); and Karim F Hirji, *The Enduring Relevance of Walter Rodney's How Europe Underdeveloped Africa*; (Mkuki Na Nyota, Dar es Salaam, 2017).

Eusi Kwayana's account of Walter Rodney's role in the WPA and the civil rebellion: *Guyana Under Siege: Walter Rodney* (1988) is available at guyanaundersiege.com/leaders/rodney3.htm

There are also a number of videos and documentaries about Walter Rodney available free online including Dr David Hinds, *In the Sky's Wild Noise: A Documentary on Dr Walter Rodney* (2014), Dwayne Omowale, *Walter Rodney-African Identity* (2016), Kilombo Uk, *Walter Rodney: Race and Class in Guyanese Politics* (2015) and Tchaiko Kwayana, *Eusi Kwayana on Walter Rodney* (2010).

For more on the Marxist approach to revolutionary politics and the theory of permanent revolution see Tony Cliff, *Deflected Permanent Revolution* and John Molyneux, *What is the real Marxist tradition?* at marxists.org